HE GOES BEFORE US
Stories From The Front Lines

GINGER SANDERS

xulon PRESS

Copyright © 2016 by Ginger Sanders

He Goes Before Us
Seeing God's Presence During Disasters – Short Stories From the Front Lines
by Ginger Sanders

Printed in the United States of America.

Library of Congress Control Number: 2013913315
ISBN 9781498459471

All rights reserved solely by the author. The author guarantees all contents are original and do not infringe upon the legal rights of any other person or work. No part of this book may be reproduced in any form without the permission of the author. The views expressed in this book are not necessarily those of the publisher.

Unless otherwise indicated, Scripture quotations taken from the New King James Version. Copyright 1979, 1980, 1982 by Thomas Nelson, inc. Used by permission. All rights reserved.

Scripture taken from the King James Version of the Bible.

Scripture quotations taken from the New American Standard Bible®, Copyright © 1960, 1962, 1963, 1968, 1971, 1972, 1973, 1975, 1977, 1995 by The Lockman Foundation. Used by permission." (www.Lockman.org)

Scriptures taken from the Holy Bible, New International Version®, NIV®. Copyright © 1973, 1978, 1984, 2011 by Biblica, Inc.™ Used by permission of Zondervan. All rights reserved worldwide. www.zondervan.com The "NIV" and "New International Version" are trademarks registered in the United States Patent and Trademark Office by Biblica, Inc.™ All rights reserved.

Scripture quotations are from the Holy Bible, English Standard Version® (ESV®), copyright © 2001 by Crossway, a publishing ministry of Good News Publishers. Used by permission. All rights reserved.

Scripture taken from the Holman Christian Standard Bible ® Copyright © 2003, 2002, 2000, 1999 by Holman Bible Publishers. All rights reserved.

Author photo courtesy of Jane Nichols Photography. Cover photo by Ginger Sanders, author.

Because of the dynamic nature of the Internet, any web addresses or links contained in this book may have changed since publication and may no longer be valid.

www.xulonpress.com

To my husband, Denny, who has walked the path of a righteous man, setting the example for me, our four wonderful children, Jamie, Kara, Todd and B.J. and now our grandchildren.

To my children who have prayed for this project and who are a blessing in so many ways.

To my family and friends who are so special to me and are our prayer warriors.

To all the Billy Graham Rapid Response Chaplains who are ready to respond instantly. This means you are always prayed up and ready to serve the King.

To the Billy Graham Rapid Response Team management and office staff, who are so diligent in their efforts, prayers and support. You may not always be out in the field to see some of these God stories, but you played a part by your faithful service.

To the Samaritan Purse staff and volunteers, whose work with disasters, has touched many hearts and opened doors for the gospel.

To all of our prayer warriors, we certainly could not go out into the battlefield unless "He Goes Before Us." Prayer is the most vital part of this ministry, for without Him, we can do nothing.

To my Lord and Savior, Jesus Christ, in allowing me to literally see You working in people's lives, as well as my own. Thank you for dying for me, but rising to the eternity that now lies before us. Thank you for letting us, as ordinary as we are, be a part of Your Great Plan of Salvation, that all may hear and "that this people may know that thou art the LORD God, and that thou hast turned their heart back again." 1 Kings 18:37 (KJV)

Faith building God stories from the real experiences of the Billy Graham Rapid Response Team chaplains.

Contents

Foreword ix
Introduction xi

1. Another Billy Graham Accepts Christ 1
2. The Mail Lady 5
3. A New Beginning 9
4. Laundry Washed by Volunteer, Soul Washed by Christ 13
5. Sharing Christ in Russian 15
6. Minot State University Students Prayed 17
7. Business Cards and Prayers 19
8. Business Cards and Prayers (Continued) 23
9. Blood of Jesus Is for Everyone 27
10. Smashed Tree 29
11. Ice Chest Salvation 31
12. No Barriers with God . . . Even in Jail 33
13. Not Everyone Will Call Out His Name 35
14. All Shall Hear 37
15. Bitterness Turned to Joy 39
16. Blankets + Holy Spirit = 1 Salvation 41
17. Sweet Salvations 43
18. Walking a Rough Road 47
19. The Giver Receives 49
20. Suicide and a Southern Prayer 51
21. The Language of Love 55

22. Walking to Find Jesus 59
23. Looking for Goodwill and Sharing It 61
24. Heavenly Father 63
25. Never Too Old 65
26. Scheduled for Salvation 69
27. A Sad Celebration 73
28. Wait upon the Lord 75
29. A Christmas Bell 79
30. A Child Shall Lead Them 83
31. Rededications and Renewal of Walking with Christ 85

Peace with God 87
Afterword 91
Acronyms 93
About the Author 95

Foreword

I can still remember our visits in the Sanders home as we listened to their stories of serving with the Billy Graham Evangelistic Association (BGEA) Billy Graham Rapid Response Team chaplains. They are amazing stories of God at work every time a chaplain team responded to a need. It was God's story lived out in the lives of ordinary people serving an extraordinary God.

Your heart will be made glad as you read these stories and see how God was working in the midst of the storms.

Esther Burroughs
Treasures of the Heart Ministry

Introduction

One of my favorite verses in the Bible is Jeremiah 29:11 (NIV). "'I know the plans I have for you,' declares the Lord, 'plans to prosper you and not to harm you, plans to give you hope and a future.'" My husband and I retired from our jobs, relying on this promise. There was no way we could have seen what was coming in our lives as God weaved His plan.

The Billy Graham Evangelistic Association has Billy Graham Rapid Response Team chaplains who are trained and are often sent out on a moment's notice when a manmade or natural disaster occurs. Many times, the chaplains go out alongside Samaritan's Purse to give physical, emotional, and spiritual care. On occasion and at request, they deploy in times of need, such as the Sandy Hook school and Aurora Theater shootings.

When we retired, we saw where the Billy Graham Rapid Response Team was looking for chaplains who had law enforcement, fire, and EMT experience. Since my husband had retired from thirty-one years of law enforcement and I had taught at the police academy, we filled out our applications.

Included in the application was the request for references. It was no problem putting down our pastor, who was at that time Billy Taylor, at the small country church in north Alabama. Brother Billy told the story of how he and his wife, Lois, were driving down the road when his cell phone rang. Not having a large screen on his phone, instead of seeing "Billy Graham Evangelistic Association," all he saw was "Billy Graham"! He pulled off the road and excitedly told Lois, "Billy Graham is calling me!" Then a lady came on the phone to inquire about us being actively involved in the local church. He said he was disappointed he did not get to talk to Billy Graham!

This book is about the stories that God has allowed us to see and hear while serving on the field with this wonderful and blessed organization. This is not a publicity book for the Billy Graham Evangelistic Association, Samaritan's Purse, or the Billy Graham Rapid Response Team, and it is in no way part of the ministry. It also is not a publicity book for my husband, me, or any of the Billy Graham Rapid Response chaplains, which is why in telling the stories we do not use the chaplains' names, unless they are needed to help explain the story. In some cases, names have been used with permission, and at other times, we changed the names to protect their privacy.

These stories are put here for you to see that our God is alive and well. He is the same God today as He was in days of old, performing miracles and having His part in people's lives by divine appointments. They are here for you to be encouraged and to be given hope. You will see in every instance that only God could have orchestrated the scene and what takes place. He, and He alone, is to be glorified.

His plan for our lives is just what He promised. "I have come that they may have life, and that they may have it more abundantly" (John 10:10 NKJV). I believe when we accept Jesus Christ as our Lord and Savior, we are given "life," but He wants so much more for us, His children. He wants to bless us with an "abundant" life, a life full of blessings that He puts before us every day. He wants us to be faithful to Him, listening to Him and calling out to Him.

If we are obedient to God, He promises to be with us. Many times we have prayed and without doubt, we know our God, *He goes before us*. Many times, as we head out in one direction, we find ourselves being called to another location. We tenderly say, "What you are sent there for may not be what you are sent there for," which is the reason for most of these stories. We are sent to a location for a requested, specific need, only to discover that God has His own agenda at this place.

As you, the reader, walk through the stories with us, I pray the Holy Spirit helps you feel His presence as we did while the story was unfolding in reality. May He touch your heart and life as He has done in the lives of these people and in our lives.

May you be blessed knowing that our God, who sent His Son, Jesus Christ, to die for us, still loves us enough to continue to play a part and intervene on our behalf, to give us joy, peace, comfort, and hope. What great joy to know that we have the promise of eternal life through Him. But it is with even greater joy to know that He is with us every day. Even if we did not have the promise of eternal life (which we do through the blood of Christ), it would still be worth having Christ in our lives every day. What joy! What blessings!

Deuteronomy 31:8 (NKJV): "And the Lord, He is the One who goes before you. He will be with you, He will not leave you nor forsake you; do not fear nor be dismayed."

Ephesians 5:15-17 (NASB): "Therefore be careful how you walk, not as unwise men but as wise, making the most of your time, because the days are evil. So then do not be foolish, but understand what the will of the Lord is."

Chapter 1

ANOTHER BILLY GRAHAM ACCEPTS CHRIST

"But rejoice, because your names are written in heaven."
—Luke 10:20 (NIV)

Chaplains were riding in an area that had been flooded and saw a contractor's truck with the name "Billy Graham" on it. The Samaritan's Purse team had been working next door and had spoken to the contractor earlier that week. When the chaplains visited, the contractor was working in the basement of the house, so they left a book by Rev. Billy Graham in the seat of his truck.

The chaplains felt led to go back in the same area the next day. When they saw the truck again, they decided to stop and meet Billy Graham. He was coming around the house where he had been working. He told them he was there from his home state, Idaho, and working on the houses that had been flooded. They talked to him about the Rev. Billy Graham and his belief in Jesus. *Contractor* Billy Graham said he too believed in Jesus, but when asked if he knew he was going to heaven when he died, he was not sure. The chaplains shared with him the hope, peace, and assurance of eternity, and Billy

Graham prayed to receive Christ. It was with great joy that they presented him with a Billy Graham Training Center Bible.

That evening, Billy came to eat with the Rapid Response chaplains and the Samaritan's Purse teams for dinner. After eating, they asked if anyone had anything to share. Billy Graham was the first one to stand up to tell he had accepted Christ that day. It was special, since the dinner and share time were under a tent, due to another event being inside at the church. It was pretty neat hearing Billy Graham speak outside in a tent!

Later, by his request, his wife called and talked to the chaplains. When they shared with her what had taken place and her husband accepted Jesus, she cried and said she had been praying for this. She shared that she had just gotten him to go to church with her a couple of weeks before he came to North Dakota and had prayed that he would meet someone in North Dakota to invite him to church. The chaplains and she actually laughed that her prayer may have been what made them come all the way from Alabama and him from Idaho to meet in North Dakota!

But the best part of this story today was this: Billy Graham's name was written once again in the Book of Life, but this time it was for another soul. We have heard it said many times that He knows our names. Have you ever thought about *why* He knows your name? Is it because He wrote *your* name in the Book of Life? The blood of Jesus seals the names written in the Book of Life. There is nothing you have ever done or can do to erase your name once it is written there. The Lamb's Book will be opened and those whose names are written will enter heaven.

Revelation 21:27 (KJV): "And there shall in no wise enter into it any thing that defileth, neither whatsoever worketh abomination, or maketh a lie: but they which are written in the Lamb's book of life."

He Goes Before Us

Denny praying with Contractor Billy Graham

Chapter 2

THE MAIL LADY

"Do not fear, for I am with you; do not be afraid,
for I am your God. I will strengthen you; I will hold
on to you with My righteous right hand."
—Isaiah 41:10 (NIV)

Iowa has had several floods in which Samaritan's Purse Disaster Relief Teams have responded. But one area had been hit by a tornado killing several people, and then following on its heels, about ten days later, was a big flood. The Rapid Response Team chaplains were called out to partner with Samaritan's Purse during this time.

We were two of those chaplains who responded, but we did not partner with each other as a husband and wife team. Oftentimes, we have partnered with another chaplain who is alone, so we go as a team of two men and a team of two women. This is what happened in Iowa. I sometimes think God has a sense of humor in the midst of the storms, just to show us He knows what is going on in His plan.

I happened to be partnered this time with a little lady from the Bronx. Now this may not seem unusual to you, but to a girl from the South, I wondered, *How is God going to work this out?* We had to laugh at each other due to the difference in speech, when we would kindly ask the other to repeat what had been said. The chaplain from the Bronx had never driven, nor had she ever seen the beautiful farmlands in Iowa. She was in awe of God's creation, even in the devastation.

Samaritan's Purse receives requests for help from homeowners in areas of disasters, whether it is chainsawing a downed tree, picking up debris, cleaning mud out of a house that has been flooded, or doing anything else that volunteers may possibly do to help the victims. These requests are created on a form we call a "work order," which describes the type of work, how many volunteers are needed, and which tools will be needed. The Rapid Response Team chaplains are then given a copy of the work order so they can go alongside Samaritan's Purse and visit each homeowner.

We were following the directions of the GPS, trying to locate a Samaritan's Purse team or the homeowner early one Tuesday morning. After a tornado or flooding, oftentimes the street signs are down and the houses are boarded up or entirely gone. This makes finding the location very difficult.

The GPS took us to the country—to a dirt and gravel road—where the houses had been touched by not only the tornado but also by the floodwaters. The rural mailboxes were down, and no numbers were anywhere to be seen. Several of the houses had been boarded up with plywood over the windows.

After traveling the road both directions and not seeing a Samaritan's Purse team working on any houses on this road, it was beginning to seem futile. Just as we—the Bronx chaplain and the "Southern belle," as she called me—thought of giving up, we noticed a mail truck turn onto the road. This was the answer! The postal carrier would surely know the route and the location of the house we were looking for.

We, going opposite directions, pulled up alongside the mail truck. We told the lady who we were, but she told us she had already seen the car traveling around and had noticed the magnetic sign that said, "The Billy Graham Rapid Response Team." She quickly pointed down the road to a house that was boarded up and empty, saying the folks had moved out of town to be near relatives and would not be back.

Then, talking through the window of the chaplain's car, we asked if she had had any damage at her home. With this question, the mail lady began to weep almost uncontrollably. Leaving the car parked in the middle of the road, we jumped out and went to her. She explained, in-between sobs, that her home had been hit by the tornado, leaving only the patio. When they had begun to sort through the debris, what was salvaged was put on the patio. Then the floodwater came and took everything they had found. "But this is not why I am crying," she said. "We lost my five-year-old granddaughter a month ago to a heart attack!" she sobbed.

We also noticed during this time of sharing that she kept looking at her watch. So we went to the trunk of the car and gave her some material and asked if we could pray with her. She said that would be good if we could pray for her and her family. Standing in the middle of the road, praying that the hand of God would touch and the Holy Spirit would be with this family, we had no idea of what was to follow.

We got her name, Karen Smiley, and told her we would call out her name in the chaplain prayer time that night. Karen went on her way and we did also, feeling God had put us on that road that day for her.

But God was not finished with this story, nor am I. God had plans to come that day, and He wanted to fulfill those plans. Tomorrow, you will know the rest of this story and how only God could start the healing of this family.

Do you need to start a healing in your own life? Start seeking His face for that healing to begin.

Chapter 3

A NEW BEGINNING

*"So you will find favor and good repute in the sight of
God and man. Trust in the Lord with all your heart
and do not lean on your own understanding."
—Proverbs 3:4-5 (NASB)*

Three days after meeting the mail lady, on the Friday before we were to leave for our home, the Bronx chaplain and the Southern Belle were given another work order in the last name of Hunter. We were to follow up after Samaritan's Purse had completed its work.

We drove out the dirt lane and turned in to follow it to the very end. At the last house, we saw we had the correct address, which was on the mailbox. The house looked all clean and pristine—no flood or storm damage to be seen. There appeared to be no one home, as if some normalcy had come into the home and they had even gone back to their jobs.

We decided, since no one was home, we would pray in the car, write a note to the homeowner, and leave it with some materials at the door. As we were getting out of the car to get the materials out of the trunk of the car, we heard a lawn mower coming around the house. There was a lady on the mower and she came around, weaving her way in and out of a child's swing set while mowing underneath the swings. As she made a turn, she looked our way and, looking very surprised and with a big smile, gave a big wave! This was odd, we thought. Did she know us? As she drove closer, we realized it was the mail lady! She was not in uniform and was not in the mail truck!

As she drove closer, she yelled, "Are you looking for me?" Well, we looked back at the name on the work order—"Hunter"—and told her that was who we were looking for. By this time, she had pulled up under a shade tree and said, "This is my daughter's home. That swing set was my granddaughter's that I told you about."

We walked over to the shade tree and sat underneath it as this dear grandmother showed us pictures, on her keychain, of her dear, sweet, little angel who had now gone on to heaven. She shared with us how the little girl had had heart problems and had suddenly died while at a restaurant after a fun-filled day with her family. How they had run across the street to the hospital's emergency room, carrying her in their arms, and how that the doctors had worked with the baby, to no avail, before uttering the words, "There is nothing more we can do. Your baby girl is gone."

But then, through the tears we all were shedding, we heard the rest. How the family was not able to go into the basement or the little girl's room to clean out her toys and clothing. But then the floods came, and with the floods, a Christian group of volunteer men and women with Samaritan's Purse came and took the little girl's belongings to the curb, not knowing what had happened in the past month at the home. Not knowing that the child had passed away and they were taking care of a task the family could not do.

Then, when the Samaritan's Purse volunteers completed their work, they presented a Bible to the homeowners, the parents of little Suzie, signed by everyone who had been on that worksite. The parents did not share their story with the team, not wanting them to be upset too. But they accepted the Bible gladly, knowing that these people had been sent there to do a job they themselves had not been able to do.

It just so happened that the Tuesday that we had first met the mail lady was the very day Suzie's mother began looking at the Bible she had been given; she was reading what the volunteers had written and the Scripture notations they had jotted down. Then she opened God's Word and started to read. Feeling the presence of God and the drawing of the Holy Spirit, Suzie's mother cried out to God, asking forgiveness and for Jesus to be her Lord and Savior.

The grandmother assured us that she too knew that she was a Christian. She had asked Jesus into her heart as a young girl, when her grandfather was preaching. But she had gotten away from God and asked that we pray for her husband and family. We were able to share with her the book of Isaiah, where God says He will hold on to you with His righteous hand. That God had never let her go and was waiting on her to come back to Him. The grandmother prayed that day, asking God to help her walk closer to Him and to be an example to her family.

As the cool breeze gently passed our faces, it felt as if the Holy Spirit Himself had been listening to the glorious things that had happened.

When hard times come, whom do you call on? Do you stop and listen for God? He is there through friends, neighbors, and loved ones, but most of all, He is there in the quiet times. He is waiting to hear from you, for you to share with Him. Tell Him your burdens today. Let the Spirit of God reign down on you.

Chapter 4

LAUNDRY WASHED BY VOLUNTEER, SOUL WASHED BY CHRIST

> He saw Jesus, fell facedown, and begged Him: "Lord,
> if You are willing, You can make me clean."
> —Luke 5:12 (HCSB)

Michelle and her son were living in temporary housing. While there to visit another homeowner, Billy Graham Rapid Response chaplains met Michelle near the laundry trailer. Volunteers were doing the laundry for the people who were living in the temporary shelter. The volunteers were writing Scripture on every bag of clean laundry. When Michelle saw the chaplains, she asked them about the Scripture on her bag: "John 3:16."

Michelle started to share her story with the chaplains. They talked about the Bible verse and showed her where it appeared in the little booklet titled *Steps to Peace*. They even looked up the Scripture itself. Michelle questioned the chaplains about eternity. Chaplains then shared about Jesus and His plan of salvation to Michelle. With tears rolling down her face, Michelle prayed to receive Christ.

Little things, such as writing Scripture on a bag of laundry, can cause people to think about their lives. We need to be aware that God can use the smallest to make the greatest. His Word can prick the hearts of men and women. We, ourselves, should have a daily time to spend in His Word, to ponder it and let Him speak to us.

Do you have time set aside in your day to spend with Him and reading His Word?

Chapter 5

SHARING CHRIST IN RUSSIAN

"As I began to speak, the Holy Spirit came on them as He had come on us at the beginning."
—Acts 11:15-17 (NIV)

The Billy Graham Rapid Response chaplains had visited the homeowner moments after her husband passed away and were able to be there with the family during the tender time. The Samaritan's Purse Disaster Relief team had signed a Bible and asked the chaplains to deliver it to the homeowner the following day.

When they arrived at the home to deliver the Bible, the caregiver of the man who had passed away was at the home. He is Russian. The young man ran to get his Russian Bible and a chaplain got his own Bible out of the car. While the one chaplain presented the Bible and spoke with the homeowner inside the home, Olis and the other chaplain were at the hood of the car with their Bibles. The chaplain was able to show him Scriptures and they compared Bibles. During this time, the chaplain was able to share Scriptures with him about Christ and His dying on the cross. Olis read the Scriptures in his Russian Bible and the Spirit of God spoke to him. The chaplain led this young Russian man to the Lord. (The chaplain later admitted that while he had been in college, he took the shortest line to sign up for three credit hours, and it ended up being the Russian language class.)

Note: This chaplain was not supposed to be sent out this week. The chaplain that should have been deployed had canceled last minute due to pending surgery. The chaplain who just "showed up," had called the Billy Graham Rapid Response Office and said a team from his church was coming to volunteer. He asked if they needed a chaplain or if he should come and volunteer with Samaritan's Purse.

He came to deploy as a RRT chaplain for the three days his team was scheduled: Tuesday, Wednesday, and Thursday. On Tuesday, the man who Olis cared for passed away. On Wednesday, the chaplains delivered the Bible and the chaplain who had some knowledge of the Russian language was able to share the gospel with the caregiver. This chaplain left on Thursday afternoon to go back with the volunteer team from his church. All in God's timing. To Him is the glory!

We serve an amazing God. We were wondering that week how "we" were going to manage with our team of chaplains, and God had already had the chaplain en route to fill our need. We should never try to get ahead of God; just trust Him in everything.

Is there something in your life that you have been trying to take care of yourself without fully trusting Him? Give it to Him today.

Chapter 6

MINOT STATE UNIVERSITY STUDENTS PRAYED

"For this reason also, since the day we heard this, we haven't stopped praying for you. We are asking that you may be filled with the knowledge of His will in all wisdom and spiritual understanding."
—Colossians 1:9 (NIV)

A Billy Graham Rapid Response Team chaplain was invited to speak one evening at North Dakota's Minot State University at the meeting of Chi Alpha (a Christian organization). When the chaplain found out that the praise team had some problems with their instruments and were not singing at the beginning, she requested the playing of the video on YouTube by Matthew West and his song "Strong Enough." It shows Samaritan's Purse volunteers and the Billy Graham Rapid Response Team chaplains in the aftermath of the Alabama tornadoes.

The chaplain had previously taught some financial classes and knew of hardships and the temptations of spending and borrowing money for college students. She knew how it is hard to get out of debt and stay out of debt. God cannot use and bless you if you are burdened by financial obligations. So she spoke about finances and college and then weaved in the gospel of Christ by sharing salvation stories. At the end of the meeting, sensing the presence of Holy Spirit the chaplain felt led to lead the group in the prayer of salvation. With every head bowed and eyes closed, you could hear the whispering of repeating the prayer. When asked if anyone prayed that prayer for the first time in his or her life, two male college students raised their hands. When asked if anyone prayed that prayer as a renewal of a relationship with Christ, three people raised their hands.

Afterward, the chaplains met with several students, one on one, and had prayer for their specific needs. Many students have a sense of loneliness and separation, even on a campus full of people. Moreover, this group of twenty-six felt the completeness that only God can give them. The chaplains prayed and asked them to encourage each other in prayers and reading God's Word and serving God together here on campus.

Many people talk about how badly the new generation can be, but while we are out in the world, there are still many praying youth. Yes, the young people do have more to deal with than I did growing up, with drugs and so many temptations. But when two or three gather together, it does not say how old they must be; He is there.

Pray for our young people as they take a stand for God, leading the way with their peers.

Chapter 7

BUSINESS CARDS AND PRAYERS

> "He that dwelleth in the secret place of the most High shall abide under the shadow of the Almighty. I will say of the Lord, He is my refuge and my fortress: my God; in him will I trust. Surely he shall deliver thee from the snare of the fowler, and from the noisome pestilence. He shall cover thee with his feathers, and under his wings shalt thou trust: his truth shall be thy shield and buckler."
> —Psalm 91:1-4 (KJV)

Late one afternoon while we were coming in from the field, my cell phone rang. One of Samaritan's Purse's assessors was calling to ask if I could come to his location. He had been in the flooded area and had found a lady, whose home had been condemned, living in her car, which was also inoperable due to the water.

When the Bronx chaplain and I arrived, the woman was sitting in the only spot vacant in her car, which was crammed with her belongings. She had not left her home since the flood and thought she had nowhere to go. We gave her some crackers and bottled water, since she said she had not eaten all day.

During deployments, we are usually given local numbers for shelters and food distributions. Being late in the day, I was not getting an answer at any of the numbers on the list. So I decided to find the number of the county social worker. When I called the number, a man answered, and when told of the situation, he said he was very close to our location. He soon arrived and confirmed the need for housing. However, he said, "This late in the day, I really don't have much hope of getting her in, due to all the places being full. However, I can lead you to the local Salvation Army, and with the Billy Graham Rapid Response Team blue shirt on, they just may listen to your request and let her stay." He stated that he had been there on many occasions and been turned down because of the late hour.

After convincing the woman to go for a good shower, clean bed, and a safe place, we followed the social worker to the Salvation Army. When we arrived and knocked at the door, we were asked what we needed through a small speaker box. I told the lady that I was a chaplain with the Billy Graham Rapid Response Team and she immediately came to the door. After sharing the situation and that this woman had no place to go, the lady in charge took a few moments to ponder what she had just heard. She said, "Only because you are wearing a Billy Graham blue shirt and I know you would not be here if this was not a dire need, I am going to stretch the rules and let her in for a shower and bed. I would not normally be able to do this; I want you to realize this." I assured the lady that I completely understood they had rules and certainly appreciated this exception being made.

After we got the woman settled in and we, as female chaplains, were allowed inside, we prayed with the workers and the woman we took to the Salvation Army.

Stepping back outside into the parking lot, we saw the social worker waiting beside his car. He shared with us that he knew it was of the Lord that they even opened their door to us. He shared with us that he was a Christian trying to work in a world that has been tainted with sin. He asked us to keep him in our prayers. He then started to give us his business card but stopped to turn it over and write a name on the back of it. He then handed the card to us, saying, "If you ever need anything, call me or my assistant. Her name is on the back."

We departed that evening, knowing God had just given us another blessing. We just did not know there was going to be more to the story! We arrived back at the church too late for our meeting with the chaplains, so we did not pass the information on about the social worker and kept the card that night.

However, that business card carried the weight of prayers that night. Yes, we cared and got shelter for someone in need, but the shelter of the soul was what was important to God.

He hears the prayers of His people and cares for them. He touches those to respond to their needs. He loves, and He cares. Do you need a place of refuge? He cares for you and wants to shelter you in His arms. Give Him your cares today. Pray to Him, giving Him all your burdens.

Chapter 8

BUSINESS CARDS AND PRAYERS (CONTINUED)

"As you help us by your prayers. Then many will give thanks on our behalf for the gracious favor granted us in answer to the prayers of many. Now this is our boast: Our conscience testifies that we have conducted ourselves in the world, and especially in our relations with you, with integrity and godly sincerity. We have done so, relying not on worldly wisdom but on God's grace."
—2 Corinthians 1:11-12 (NIV)

The next day, my husband and Howard, another male chaplain, went out with the anticipation of delivering a Bible, which had been signed by the volunteers, to a homeowner. After much searching, they were told the man was not at home but was possibly at a local nursing home. They both said they felt excitement about why they were being sent to this nursing home, thinking, *There must be a reason for this. The man is not a Christian, and we are going to get to lead him to the Lord!*

When they arrived at the nursing home, just knowing they were going to win this gentleman to Christ, they found him in his room—with his well-worn Bible open in his lap. He was doing his morning devotions. He had been a Christian for many years. Needless to say, this team of chaplains was glad to meet him, but just a bit disappointed in what *they* thought was to be a divine appointment. They gave the man his signed Bible and had a wonderful visit with him, ending it in prayer.

They walked out of his room, dejectedly, asking what had happened. What they thought would happen just did not happen! They still had a burden, but they did not understand why or where it was coming from!

They walked on down the hallway, entering the waiting room area. As they did, a lady working on a clipboard passed them and they nodded as they spoke to her. She walked past a few steps and she hollered back, "Samaritan's Purse!" The Billy Graham Rapid Response chaplains told her, "Yes, we work alongside Samaritan's Purse." She expressed to them how grateful she was that so many people had come to volunteer and to help her town. She didn't know what they would have done without the help.

The chaplains asked her what church she attended, and she replied, "I have been in a church, but I have been disillusioned with my religion for years." When the chaplains asked her if she would like to take care of that, she replied, "Yes, I would like to do that." While continuing to speak with her, it was clear that this lady had never had a personal relationship with Christ. The chaplains explained to her how she could pray and receive Christ as her personal Savior. The lady said she felt this was something she needed to do. So sitting in the lobby of the nursing home, the chaplains led this lady in prayer of forgiveness and acceptance of Christ.

After praying, the lady said she would like to give them her business card, so that if they ever needed anything, they could call her.

The chaplains came back to the church, overjoyed that God had a plan all of His own that day. It wasn't what the chaplains expected, but God had it all worked out. For you see, when the chaplains met for their nightly meeting, the plan began to unfold and reveal itself. When the male chaplains told their story for the day, they pulled out the business card of the nursing-home lady who had received Christ that day. This reminded me of the business card that I had received the night before from the social worker. I dug down into my bag to retrieve it and handed it to our chaplain coordinator that night. As she received both business cards, a strange and puzzled look came upon her face. She looked up at us and stated, "These are from the same place!" We were puzzled too! We looked at the cards and the lady they had led to the Lord that day was the same name that had been written on the back of the card from the night before.

The man who was her boss basically wrote her name down the night before. He had told of struggles working in an environment of non-Christians. God had put her in the place the very next day, where our chaplains were to be on a mission delivering a God's Word in print and were able to share God's Word in another's heart. I feel sure this lady had been influenced by her supervisor in her office, and somehow, I think she shared with him what change had taken place in her life.

God's plan is better than our own. We can see amazing things happen, if we just stay in tune, and if we let go and let God.
What is God's plan for your life? Are you "in tune?"

Birmingham Tornado April 2011

Chapter 9

BLOOD OF JESUS IS FOR EVERYONE

> "But now in Christ Jesus, you who were once far away
> have been brought near by the blood of Jesus."
> —Ephesians 2:13 (NIV)

Billy Graham Rapid Response chaplains stopped by a seventy-six-year-old woman's home whose trees had been removed by Samaritan's Purse volunteers. The sweet woman invited the chaplain inside to sit on the sofa. The chaplain asked her had she been home during the storm and her eyes got big and she said, "Oh my, yes!" The chaplain listened to her explain in some detail of what had happened as she heard the storm outside her home. The chaplain asked her did she know for sure, if she had died that night, would she have gone to heaven. The woman said, "I am a Jehovah Witness, but I do not know for sure that I would go to heaven."

She told the chaplain that the Samaritan's Purse volunteers had given her a Bible and that she had been reading it the past several nights. The chaplain told her that Jesus came to die for our sins and rose again, to conquer death, to give us eternal home in heaven. The woman asked what is the difference between God and Jesus and the chaplain shared that Jesus is the Son of God that gave His life for us. That God the Father sent His Son so that we would not perish, but have eternal life. Moreover, that after Jesus went back to heaven, He sent the Holy Spirit to be with us until we go to be with Him.

The chaplain explained that it is hard to believe without faith; we must have faith and trust. The woman said, "I believe what you tell me." The chaplain said to her, "If you believe these things, that Jesus, the Son of God, died on the cross for your sins and rose again, then if you confess with your mouth, your sins and ask forgiveness, you shall go to heaven when you die. It has been promised to us. Would you like to pray?" The elderly woman, with tears in her eyes, prayed and asked forgiveness of her sin and Jesus to be her Lord and Savior! She and the chaplain hugged and cried together, now sisters in Christ, skin color and age did not separate the two, for the Blood of Jesus is for everyone.

Religion is simply the name of what we call the "ritual" of our beliefs. Religion is not the road to heaven. It is only the faith and belief in Jesus and His death, burial and resurrection that is the road to heaven. Going to church and works are good things, but those things are to help us grow in Him, not to lead us to Him. The Bible says, "Jesus answered, "I am the way and the truth and the life. No one comes to the Father except through me." John 14:6 NIV 1984

Do you believe these things? Are you playing at religion? Do you know for sure of your eternal home?

Chapter 10

SMASHED TREE

> "Do not be conformed to this world, but be transformed
> by the renewing of your mind, that you may prove what is
> that good and acceptable and perfect will of God."
> —Romans 12:2 (NKJV)

After stopping to visit a homeowner, chaplains noticed two men, ages twenty and thirty-two, sitting on the front porch. The homeowner was their grandmother, who had shared Jesus with them as young boys.

A chaplain exchanged small talk with the men and then noticed a car that had been smashed and destroyed by a tree during the storm. He told one of the men, "Someday day *your tree* may come. Are you ready to meet your maker?"

The young man sat up tall and straight and said he was not ready to die. The chaplain explained to them, "We are all going to die unless the Lord comes back first. Either way, we need to be ready." He then asked if they would like to take care of that right now; they both said for the chaplain to keep on telling them what to do.

The chaplain explained very simply the plan of salvation, and then he asked to have the honor in leading them in a prayer. Both of these young men, after listening intently to the words the chaplain spoke, bowed their heads and prayed to accept Christ. The chaplain presented a Bible to both of them and encouraged them to attend the local church and share with their family, especially their grandmother, what they had done.

People have heard of young children dying while saying they were "too young" or elderly people saying they "lived a full life." But it is not the length of time spent on this earth that is going to make the difference in eternity. It is your relationship with Jesus Christ and believing He died for you.

Life on earth is short, whether it is a long one or not. My mother once said, "The older you get, the faster time goes by." Well, time goes at the same speed, but we begin to realize it does go quickly. Yet eternity will go forever and ever. We all will have "our own tree" to face one day.

Are we ready to meet our maker? What about your loved ones? Do they know about Jesus? Pray that He will give you words of wisdom as someone comes across your path, so that you can share with him or her.

Denny leading two young men to Christ

Chapter 11

ICE CHEST SALVATION

> "And the peace of God, which surpasses every thought,
> will guard your hearts and minds in Christ Jesus."
> —Philippians 4:7 (HCSB)

One day while driving through disaster area, Billy Graham Rapid Response chaplains noticed an elderly lady sitting in the shade by her flooded home, having lunch off the top of an ice chest. As they pulled into a driveway down the street, the other chaplain asked, "What are you doing?" He smiled and said, "You know we are supposed to stop and talk to her." Turning around, they went back to visit with the lady.

The woman, named Martha, shared about the flood and how she was now displaced. She shared with the chaplains that she and her husband had been married over fifty years and had lived in this house for over thirty-five years. Then a chaplain asked Martha about her eternal home. She replied, "Well, I hope I go to heaven, but I don't know for sure." A chaplain replied, "God loves you and sent His son to die for you." She surprised them when she said she had heard of Jesus but did not know He had died for her!

Sitting down on the ground beside Martha, they gently went through the *Steps of Peace* with her, showing her how she could know for sure that she could spend eternity in heaven. She listened intently and then asked, "What must I do?"

Martha then bowed her head and prayed, confessing that she was a sinner. She asked Jesus to forgive her and to come into life as her Lord and Savior.

Martha, at the young age of eighty-one, gladly took the Billy Graham Training Center Bible so she could learn more of the peace and hope that Jesus gives.

She smiled and waved good-bye, hugging her new Bible as they drove away. There was now a peace on her face that replaced the sorrow and hopelessness that had been there before.

It is true that the mission field is not the other side of the world. The mission field is where we are, sometimes in our own community. As you leave our church parking lot, there is a sign that reads, "You are now entering the mission field." Wherever we are, we are to be missionaries.

What are your plans today to be a missionary? Pray that God will use you today.

Chapter 12

NO BARRIERS WITH GOD... EVEN IN JAIL

"It is better to trust in the Lord than to put confidence in man."
—Psalm 118:8 (KJV)

Mary attended the Sunday services at the host church, where the chaplains were staying due to the flood. During the week, she was arrested for various charges and was also dealing with probation violations. The Billy Graham Rapid Response chaplains decided to visit her in jail, but upon arriving they were told, "There are no visiting hours today."

God did a mighty work in the hearts of the men in authority, so the chaplains were granted visiting privileges. They were separated by glass and talked through phones, but still they had a meaningful visit. While holding the *Steps to Peace with God* booklet up to the window, Mary read the prayer to rededicate her life to Christ. The chaplains left some reading materials for her with the guard.

The chaplains are not sure whether Mary received the materials that were left, but knowing the awesome God we serve, they are sure of one thing: whoever was supposed to have gotten them that day, did!

We do not know the future for Mary or what happens in the hearts of man, but we do know that God listens and hears and answers our prayers. He has a plan, and if we look closely enough, we can see just a subtle hint of it as we walk on this earth.

We should turn to the Lord with all supplications and lean on Him in times of need.

God has a plan for everyone. His main purpose is that we know Him and have a personal relationship with Him. Then He expects us to learn and grow in Him. This can be done by reading His Word and knowing Him. Do you know God's plan for you? Are you certain His ways are your ways? If you are not sure, stop right now and talk to Him. He is waiting on you.

Chapter 13

NOT EVERYONE WILL CALL OUT HIS NAME

*"But God shows his love for us in that while we
were still sinners, Christ died for us."*
—Romans 5:8 (ESV)

Chaplains went to a home to deliver a Samaritan's Purse Bible. At the request of the wife, the volunteers did not give the Bible to her; she wanted it presented to her husband.

Samaritan's Purse volunteers sometimes request to ride with the chaplains and see how that side of the ministry goes. Chaplains had a man unexpectedly ask permission to come with them.

When they arrived at the home, the husband was alone and it was apparent he was not expecting them. Nevertheless, he was gracious and invited them into the home that had been damaged by the storm; the husband and wife were trying to live in the remains.

While talking to the man, he started to share his story about the storm, with tears running down his face, and then he admitted he needed help. The volunteer recognized the symptoms, because he had dealt with the same issues several years before. (God is amazing bringing just the right people together in their time of need!) The

Samaritan's Purse volunteer spoke up and asked him, "You are an alcoholic, aren't you?" The man, broken, admitted he was.

The chaplains shared about how God loves him and forgives all sin, that all sin is equal in God's eyes. But the man stated he was not ready to pray and ask forgiveness. His eyes looked pleadingly into the eyes of the chaplains; almost like an unspoken "help me." He would not let go of the tight hold this demon of alcohol had on him.

After praying with him, he continued to hold steadfast and would not let go and submit to the Spirit of God that was present in that storm-battered place. Chaplains just visited with him and loved on him. When he asked if they could come back another day, they assured him that they would be praying for him and would visit his home before leaving town in a few weeks.

Please pray for this man, Tim, so that he will know that you do not need to be perfect before accepting Christ. Christ says, "Come as you are and your sins will be forgiven."

Chapter 14

ALL SHALL HEAR

"And I, if I be lifted up from the earth, will draw all men unto me."
—John 12:32 (KJV)

A Billy Graham Rapid Response chaplain was talking with an Aurora police officer at the memorial site adjacent to the theater where the mass shooting had occurred, when he noticed a young woman sobbing uncontrollably.

After he finished speaking with the officer, the chaplain approached the woman. She said her name was Christy, and the chaplain asked if she knew any of the victims personally. She replied, "No." She stated that she was just at a very crucial time of her life and that it made her more sensitive to the senseless loss of life that had occurred here. The chaplain asked if he could inquire as to what it is that she was going through. Christy shared that she was the mother of five children and that she was scheduled for major brain surgery in August. She said she was sure that the doctors knew what "should be done" and are well prepared, but she was aware of the dangers.

The chaplain shared the hope that we have in Jesus. He spoke of the God who knows her condition and her fears. He added that our God has purpose in all things, including Christy's life, and that He wants to be a part of the process through which she was going.

The chaplain offered to pray for her emotional and physical health, but first he asked Christy two important questions. "You said that you are aware of the dangers of the operation. But are you prepared for the reality that you might not survive the operation? Do you think that if you were to die in the operating room, or even today, you would go to heaven?" To the first, she responded, "Yes." To the second, she said that she thought so, because she had "faith the size of a mustard seed."

The chaplain assured Christy that she could be 100 percent sure of her eternity and shared the gospel with her. Still sobbing, she said that she would love to have that security, to which the chaplain responded by offering to lead her in prayer. So holding hands in the middle of the multitude gathered at that memorial, they prayed together. First, that God would take care of all medical-related issues prior to and during the operation and long recovery. In addition, that He would give her peace as she prepared for that day. Secondly, Christy prayed while repenting of her sin, recognizing Christ's gift at the cross and receiving Him in her heart as Lord and Savior.

Now Christy, noticeably composed and with a smile on her face, gave repeated thanks to the chaplain. She finished by saying, "You came all the way from Puerto Rico. I was on my way to buy an ice cream and felt the need to stop here at the memorial. And I am so glad that I met you."

The chaplain shared his appreciation for her having shared so much and gave Christ the glory for her new life and peace found in Him.

When we see someone hurting, we often are too busy to stop. We are so busy with our own lives that we don't have time for others, even for God, who has put them there for a reason.

Be more alert to who is placed in your life as you go out into the world. Is there someone God wants you to talk with? Listen to the drawing of the Spirit.

Chapter 15

BITTERNESS TURNED TO JOY

> "What do you think? If a man owns a hundred sheep, and one
> of them wanders away, will he not leave the ninety-nine on
> the hills and go to look for the one that wandered off?"
> —Matthew 8:12 (NIV)

When the Billy Graham Rapid Response chaplains arrived at a worksite after the storm, they noticed a man who was cleaning up his yard several houses down. Feeling led to walk down to meet him, the man told the chaplains he did not need any help. Besides, he said, it was rental property and he wouldn't get any if he asked.

He seemed bitter in the beginning, but slowly he started to cheer up as the conversation moved on and he shared his story. He actually became very cheerful as time went by.

The chaplains asked him if he had a personal relationship with Christ. He felt that he had received Christ as a child but had strayed in the last fifty years. Since the storm had come so close to his home, he realized life and death are only moments apart. He said he had been thinking about death and God and it was time to make peace with Him. The chaplains told him God was waiting on him. The man prayed to rededicate his life to God. He said he felt God had spared him and was giving him a new beginning.

He said that cleaning up in the yard had been a blessing, since the chaplains came down to him. Not only was his yard now clean, but also his life had been made anew.

Has the Spirit of God been nudging you to speak to someone? Maybe renew a relationship or make a new friend with a neighbor who you see out in their yard every week? Christ blesses those who give of themselves to draw others back to Him.

Let His love shine through you.

Chapter 16

BLANKETS + HOLY SPIRIT = 1 SALVATION

> "For all things are for your sakes, so that the grace which
> is spreading to more and more people may cause the
> giving of thanks to abound to the glory of God."
> —2 Corinthians 4:15 (NASB)

Samaritan's Purse office manager from Denver, Colorado, asked the Billy Graham Rapid Response chaplains to deliver handmade, crocheted lap blankets from people in her church to a nursing home. Chaplains got the blankets and randomly found a local nursing home to give them away. The receptionist gladly accepted them for the patients. The chaplains told her who they were and how the blankets had gotten to Minot.

In the conversation, the chaplains asked her if she believed in Jesus, and she nodded yes. Then the chaplain asked her, "If you died today, would you go to heaven?"

She bowed her head and quietly replied, "No."

The chaplain sat down by the receptionist and explained how she could know she would have eternal life in heaven. The receptionist listened, tears in her eyes, and then prayed, asking Jesus into her heart.

The phone was ringing on the desk and the chaplain told her, "You may answer the phone." She smiled while saying, "I am not supposed to be here for another hour; someone else is answering these calls."

You see God's timing in all things? These are not just coincidences. Chaplains would not have even been in the nursing home, had it not been for the blanket delivery. And the lady coming into work an hour early that day? Only God can orchestrate such things!

Blankets made in Denver, brought by Samaritan's Purse worker from Colorado, given to a random nursing home in North Dakota, to a receptionist who wasn't supposed to be there, by a Billy Graham Rapid Response chaplain from Alabama who was called because of floods to share Jesus . . . All of this plus the Holy Spirit (from heaven) = 1 salvation (for His glory)!

God can use any and every person to play a part in His great plan! To see how only He can put all the pieces together and see, in His timing, all things work to bring glory to Him. In these things, we must be obedient to answer the call and make, go, and share whatever He asks us to do.

What is God calling you to do today?

Chapter 17

SWEET SALVATIONS

*"As for Me, if I am lifted up from the earth
I will draw all people to Myself."
—John 12:32 (HCSB)*

Billy Graham Rapid Response Team chaplains had been out at the Sandy Hook memorials and outside in line at a wake for one of the shooting victims. The chaplains were wet and cold from the rain. Before heading back to the hotel, they decided to stop for coffee and treats, since they had not eaten dinner. Stopping at a Dunkin' Donuts shop, chaplains went in and walked by a rowdy group of young adults. As chaplains smiled and greeted them, they apologized to the chaplains for being so loud. Chaplains commented to them, "It is good to share laughter with friends."

Chaplains ordered and went to the back of the shop to eat and relax. As they finished eating, the chaplains heard music for the first time since they had arrived. Had the young people quieted or had someone just turned it on? It was "Amazing Grace," and it was coming from the front of the shop where they sat. Chaplains got up and moved toward them, thinking someone was playing it on their phone, when they noticed a television on the wall. On the television were the pictures of the slain and the music of "Amazing Grace," as silence had gripped the shop.

The chaplains asked if anyone knew any of the victims. One said the little girl now on the screen was his neighbor.

Chaplains listened to the stories of the young adults, one of them being about their eighteen-year-old friend who had been tragically killed two weeks prior, after being hit by a truck. Chaplains told them, "We are all going to die one day. We need to have a relationship with Jesus so that we will be ready when that day comes. God loves all of us so much He sent His son to die for us."

The chaplains explained that if you believe Jesus came, died for you, and rose again, then all that is left to do is confess you sins and ask Him to be your Lord and Savior. You will be saved and will spend eternity in heaven.

The chaplain said to them, "You don't have to be in church to do this. Jesus did not die on a cross in church, nor was He born in a church. He comes to you where you are." They told the young adults they were going outside and if anyone wanted to talk to them, to come outside. Before going out, the chaplains asked to pray with them. They all said that would be good. The chaplains prayed a prayer of comfort and peace for them and this community.

Chaplains exited the shop and slowly walked toward their vehicle. Along the way, they noticed not just one or two get up, but a group came to the door and went to stand on the sidewalk. Chaplains went back to the group. As the chaplains approached, one young lady asked for her phone number, another said, "Can I have it also?" And then another. The chaplains felt they all were wanting more information and felt the Spirit of God tugging at their hearts.

The chaplains talked to them briefly about how, when you pray to receive Christ, your sins are forgiven and your name is written in the Book of Life. Nothing you have ever done or will do can erase your name. It is sealed by the blood of Jesus. She then asked them if they would like to pray, and several nodded their heads. The chaplains, standing in the circle of these young adults, led them in the Sinner's Prayer. Then they asked the young people how many had prayed that prayer for the first time in their life. Seven hands went up.

There had been one man inside that was a Christian and he had stayed over on the other side of the sidewalk, diverting a couple of females from coming over. After the prayers, he came over and spoke to the chaplains, shaking their hands and saying, "Thank you so much for being here for my friends." He had been praying for these young adults for several years.

The young adults told the chaplains that after they had walked away to purchase their food, they had been talking about how nice the chaplains had been; the chaplains had even stopped to talk with them. One said, "No one here would have done that. It was true Southern hospitality."

However, we know it was the presence of the Holy Spirit.

Is your name written in the Book of Life? Have you prayed to receive Christ as your Savior? He listens to our prayers and wants us to be drawn unto Him. If you don't know Him, today is the day of salvation. If you know Him, is there someone you can pray for or share the love of Christ with today?

Be led by His presence.

Chapter 18

WALKING A ROUGH ROAD

> "Come to me, all you who are weary and
> burdened, and I will give you rest."
> Matthew 11:28 (NIV)

Elizabeth was a well-dressed, attractive lady. When she was walking from a block away, I noticed her. Then, as she got closer, I noticed tears running down her cheeks. When I walked up beside her and asked if she was going to be okay, she nodded. But then she replied, "A man a few blocks back, with a blue shirt on just like the one you have on, prayed for me. I have never had anyone pray for me before. It really touched me, and I am not sure why I am crying."

Just walking beside her, listening to her share through her quiet sobs, seemed to give her comfort.

After walking along with her for about a block, I asked if she knew Jesus Christ as her Savior and she said, "No, can you help me?"

Elizabeth's heart had been touched by a kind word of prayer; the Holy Spirit had been knocking on her heart for those few blocks. She just needed the guidance of how to pray and accept Christ. God had placed all of us right where He wanted us that day, scattered along her path, on a hot sidewalk in New Orleans.

This is the way it is in life. We as Christians are scattered in the lives of others, and we just need to be there with a kind word and a prayer.

Do you need to say a kind word to someone today? Maybe say a prayer or just be there to walk along a rough patch of life with them. Encourage someone, and let him or her see Jesus in you.

Chapter 19

THE GIVER RECEIVES

"God is our refuge and strength, a very present help in trouble."
—Psalm 46:1 (KJV)

The chaplains were asked to deliver a signed Bible to an elderly homeowner by Samaritan's Purse. When they arrived, they found a very fit, eighty-year-old gentleman who at the time was a volunteer fireman.

He was anxious to share his story of being out volunteering and helping rescue the night Hurricane Sandy hit the east coast. Chaplains listened as he shared his story of how his own wife had fallen into the swirling waters, as the boat came to rescue her.

Both husband and wife had survived the storm, but they faced a night of terror and near death. The Billy Graham chaplains then asked him if he was sure of where he would spend eternity if he had died that night. He lowered his head and said he knew of Jesus but did not know for sure about his eternal home. They shared with him the gospel of Christ. The chaplains had the honor to lead this elderly volunteer firefighter in the Sinner's Prayer.

In the midst of storms, people often turned to Jesus. It is never too late to seek Him. He truly is our refuge and strength, but even more, He is our Savior!

Praise Him for the gift that truly saves us from death!

Chapter 20

SUICIDE AND A SOUTHERN PRAYER

"The effective, fervent prayer of a righteous man avails much."
—James 5:16 (NKJV)

One evening, after dinner, the Billy Graham Rapid Response chaplains were standing in the dining area when one of the Samaritan's Purse volunteers frantically came by and grabbed a chaplain by the arm and pulled her into the hallway. The sobbing female volunteer told the chaplain that her twenty-nine-year-old son had called to tell her good-bye. He was going to commit suicide.

The chaplain immediately placed her hands on the shoulders of the broken mother and earnestly prayed for God to intervene and let this young man know that not only did the mother love him, but so does Jesus.

After minutes of pleading with God, the chaplain noticed the mother still holding the phone up to her chest. The chaplain asked, "Is he still on the phone?" The mother nodded yes, that she had run to get her and had not hung up. The phone, someway during this time, had been put on speakerphone. The chaplain introduced herself over the phone to the young man, whose name was Mike. He said he had heard the prayer and believed God was present with him.

The chaplain talked to the young man for some time on the phone, asking him to call a church close by him, since he was out of town. During this time, the chaplain was also on her personal phone, trying to find a church, and was able to give him phone numbers in addition to the toll-free suicide number. The chaplain asked Mike, "If you are going to die today, would you go to heaven?" He assured her that he knew he was saved and would go to heaven.

The chaplain told him that there was a place for him, as a Christian, in God's plan and asked him to read Jeremiah 29:11-12. He promised he would read that after hanging up. The chaplain also got him to promise to call her tomorrow and let her hear from him the results of the phone calls he would make.

That evening, a volunteer showed up at camp from the same town Mike lived in. (Another God thing!) The chaplain knew the volunteer and was able to ask him if he knew of a good Christian counselor in that area. He not only gave a name and number but also called him, and the chaplain spoke with him. He was a pastor at a church that was only blocks from where Mike lived. He said he would love to speak with him and would not charge any fees; this was truly a divine appointment!

Mike did call the chaplain the next day and told her how much he appreciated her being there for him, as well as his mother. He had not been able to reach anyone at any of the churches the night before but stated that reading God's Word in Jeremiah really helped him. He did say that he had received a call from the counselor that morning and would be meeting with him that very day.

His mother confirmed today that he was doing better and he had also told her that he had make the appointment to seek help. She was so appreciative of the chaplain being available, but we look back and see how God orchestrated everyone being in place to aid this young man.

The mother did share with the chaplain that when he talked to her later, he told her he had almost freaked out the night before when he called his mother. He thought his mother had started to earnestly pray with a Southern accent! It certainly had gotten his attention!

God can use all things to His glory to get our attention! That night was proof of His timing and using our tongues! Think back on the times in your life that God showed up unexpectedly and you now realize it could have only been Him! He loves us very much—we often are not even aware of His presence. Be careful in your life to give Him glory and realize He is wants to take care of us, not to harm us.
Praise Him who created us and loved us so much to send His Son and the Holy Spirit.

Chapter 21

THE LANGUAGE OF LOVE

"For even as the body is one and yet has many members, and all the members of the body, though they are many, are one body, so also is Christ. For by one Spirit we were all baptized into one body, whether Jews or Greeks, whether slaves or free, and we were all made to drink of one Spirit. For the body is not one member, but many. If the foot says, "Because I am not a hand, I am not a part of the body," it is not for this reason any the less a part of the body. And if the ear says, "Because I am not an eye, I am not a part of the body," it is not for this reason any the less a part of the body. If the whole body were an eye, where would the hearing be? If the whole were hearing, where would the sense of smell be? But now God has placed the members, each one of them, in the body, just as He desired. If they were all one member, where would the body be? But now there are many members, but one body. And the eye cannot say to the hand, "I have no need of you"; or again the head to the feet, "I have no need of you." On the contrary, it is much truer that the members of the body which seem to be weaker are necessary; and those members of the body which we deem less honorable, on these we bestow more abundant honor, and our less presentable members become much more presentable, whereas our more presentable members have no need of it. But God has so composed the body, giving more abundant honor to that member which lacked, so that there may be no division in the body, but that the members may have the same care for one another. And if one member suffers, all the members suffer with it; if one member is honored, all the members rejoice with it."
—1 Corinthians 12:12-26 (NASB)

One day, a Samaritan's Purse Team leader was driving and saw an elderly Japanese lady dragging a heavy garbage can to the road and stopped to offer help. Finding that she had been flooded and her children had helped her clean and mud-out her home, the SP leader offered for SP to come and power-wash and do mold remediation.

The spray team arrived and started cleaning the basement. While there, one of the SP members talked with the lady and found out she had married a US Army man after the war and came to America from Japan. She taught herself English but still spoke with a strong, broken accent.

The next morning, one of the Samaritan's Purse volunteers came and asked the Billy Graham Rapid Response chaplains if they had a Japanese Bible. One of the chaplains is also a Gideon and immediately thought of them. Looking in the phone book, he called the number for the local Gideon's and asked if they had a Japanese Bible. The Gideon, Mr. Clark, said he did have a Japanese-English Bible he used for speaking in churches and he was willing to give it to the Billy Graham Rapid Response chaplains.

The chaplains drove out, across the beautiful farm country, to the Gideon's home and farm. Mr. Clark told the chaplains he had no idea why he had this Bible, which had a column of Japanese and a correlating column of English on the same page. He said he was not even sure what language it was until they had called and he had looked in the front of the Bible. Mr. Clark was pleased we had found him and he had just what was needed. The chaplains circled on the porch of the farmhouse and prayed with Mr. Clark over the Bible, thanking God for leading them to it and blessing it for His purpose.

They took the Japanese-English Bible to the job site, where Riko lived. They called down to the basement and gave the Bible to the team leader and then went to talk with Riko.

Riko said she was seventy-six years old and was raised in the Buddhist culture. She shared about the flood and getting older and her husband dying. When they asked her if she believed in Jesus Christ, she said she had attended the Lutheran church in high school and she believed in Him, but she was not sure of heaven. They shared the love of Jesus and the hope and assurance He can give for eternity. Riko, in broken English, prayed to receive Jesus Christ as her Lord and Savior.

Everyone signed the Bible, along with the SP team, and the Japanese-English Bible was given to Riko. She can now read more about the salvation and promises and hope Jesus has for her.

God uses many parts of the body, and He is glorified!

Little things in life—helping a neighbor, sharing a book, teaching someone to read God's Word—all have a purpose and a part in spreading the gospel of Christ. Little things can be made big in the eyes of God, especially when they lead to someone coming to know His Son.

Look today. Pray for opportunities to do one little thing for someone, in the name of Jesus.

Chapter 22

WALKING TO FIND JESUS

> "And you shall seek me, and find me, when you
> shall search for me with all your heart."
> —Jeremiah 29:13 (KJV)

A couple of the Billy Graham Rapid Response Team chaplains were making a follow-up visit with homeowners who had been helped by Samaritan's Purse. A young mother and her son passed by while walking their dog. The chaplains felt compelled to offer her books and explained how they were there for people going through hard times.

As the discussion centered on "hope" and where people place their hope, the young mother said she could relate to the temporal, unstable nature of things of this world. The chaplains shared with her how God is there for everyone. Patti said she needed peace and hope and explained how her life had been very unstable the past few years. Then she said the storm came and things seemed to just get harder. Patti listened as the chaplains explained about the peace and hope that Christ can give her. Her troubles will not disappear, but Christ will be there to comfort her.

Patti told the chaplains she would like to pray the prayer of salvation and receive Christ. Patti prayed, and she had a new look on her face, one of peace and contentment, which had not been there before. As she went her way, she had a big smile when she turned back to wave.

When we go out, as chaplains, we are more aware and in tune with the Spirit. Is it because of all the prayer warriors? Is it because we are feeling His presence? Sure, I am positive both of these play a big part of what we see and hear. But when we are not deployed, we tend to not pay as much attention. This is not right in God's eyes. We need to always be aware of Him and His plan as He leads people to us.

Please pray for the Billy Graham Rapid Response chaplains today so that we, along with you, will be more sensitive in our daily walk with Him. Pray that we will be on guard to the hurdles in life but also will be encouraged to share the precious story of Jesus.

Chapter 23

LOOKING FOR GOODWILL AND SHARING IT

> And said, "Cornelius, your prayer has been heard, and your
> acts of charity have been remembered in God's sight."
> —Acts 10:31(HCSB)

The Billy Graham Rapid Response chaplains were just getting ready to leave their host for the Binghamton floods, Davis Bible College, for the morning. They were still in the parking lot when a man drove up to donate a box of pots and pans. He was going to be leaving town that afternoon and would not have the time to look for a donation location, so they took the box and offered to donate them for him.

After driving around a couple of days, with pans rattling in the trunk of the car, they decided it was time to look for a Goodwill Store. Seeing an elderly lady working in her yard, one of the chaplains got out to ask about a local thrift store or Goodwill that would accept donations. The lady did not know of one but continued to share with the chaplain about the flood and her recent fall down several steps, resulting in four large staples in her head. She then saw "Billy Graham Rapid Response Team" on the chaplain's shirt and remarked how her husband used to watch Mr. Graham on television all the time.

Feeling led to ask, the chaplain asked Mrs. Irene if she had not survived the fall, would she know that she would go to the heaven that Billy Graham preached about? She said, "No, I am a Catholic and I am not sure you can know."

She listened as the chaplain was able to explain the Scripture. 1 John 5:12-13 says, "You may know that you have eternal life."

After the chaplain asked if she could share something, Mrs. Irene stepped closer and the chaplain shared the gospel of Christ with her, using the *Steps to Peace* brochure. Before the chaplain could even read the Salvation Prayer to her at the end, she started to pray, asking forgiveness and asking Jesus to come into her life.

Ms. Irene smiled and waved as the chaplains drove away.

Goodwill and mercy were found in the driveway of Ms. Irene's home!

As the chaplains drove around the corner, a Goodwill Donation Center was there!

Even in our daily lives of rattling pans, we find that Jesus can use all things to get our attention. The donor never will know on this earth, unless he is the reader, how God used his gift of pots and pans to give the gift of salvation. Won't it be wonderful when we all can get to heaven and the "rest of the stories" are reveled to us?

Do you have "beginnings" in your life that you wonder how they ended? What a joyous time in heaven it will be!

Chapter 24

HEAVENLY FATHER

> "And whatsoever ye do in word or deed, do all in the name of the Lord Jesus, giving thanks to God and the Father by him."
> —Colossians 3:17 (KJV)

One day Billy Graham Rapid Response chaplains went out to a Samaritan's Purse team for prayer and the homeowner was there helping. He was not supposed to be there, but God had a plan.

When the Samaritan's Purse team first arrived at the worksite, a neighbor walked over and told one of the team leaders that she thought this house was a rental and they were at the wrong address. Therefore, the team leader called back to the SP disaster unit to confirm the address. The SP office contacted the homeowner and was assured this was their residence and the address was correct. The wife asked when they would be arriving. Being told they were already there, she said she would call her husband because he wanted to be there to help them.

The chaplains arrived as the team was just taking a break and spoke with the homeowner. Sitting on a turned over five-gallon bucket, the homeowner shared with the chaplains as the team went back to work. He started telling about the flood, but then tearing up, he shared about his dad dying in a tragic plane crash when he was only four years old. He shared how hard that had been on his mom as he was growing up and that he grew up without a dad.

They talked to him about Jesus and the peace and hope He can give. He listened and said he would like to receive that peace. They were able to tell him about the promise of eternal life and a security and hope. He listened, and then he bowed his head and prayed a sweet prayer to receive forgiveness and salvation. They then shared that he now has a heavenly Father that he can talk to anytime, one that loves him very much and will be with him.

Through his tears, he smiled and looked up. I am sure his heavenly Father was looking down.

Christ does not promise us that our life on earth will be easy, but He does promise us He will be with us.

Do you need to lean on Him today, give Him your burden? He is waiting on you, my friend. He never forsakes us. God loves you so very much.

Chapter 25

NEVER TOO OLD

An angel of the Lord spoke to Philip: "Get up and go south to the road that goes down from Jerusalem to Gaza." (This is the desert road.) So he got up and went. There was an Ethiopian man, a eunuch and high official of Candace, queen of the Ethiopians, who was in charge of her entire treasury. He had come to worship in Jerusalem and was sitting in his chariot on his way home, reading the prophet Isaiah aloud. The Spirit told Philip, "Go and join that chariot." When Philip ran up to it, he heard him reading the prophet Isaiah, and said, "Do you understand what you're reading?" "How can I," he said, "unless someone guides me?" So he invited Philip to come up and sit with him. Now the Scripture passage he was reading was this:

> "He was led like a sheep to the slaughter,
> and as a lamb is silent before its shearer,
> so He does not open His mouth.
> In His humiliation justice was denied Him.
> Who will describe His generation?
> For His life is taken from the earth."

The eunuch replied to Philip, "I ask you, who is the prophet saying this about—himself or another person?" So Philip proceeded to tell him the good news about Jesus, beginning from that Scripture. As they were traveling down the road, they came to some water. The eunuch said, "Look, there's water! What would keep me from being

baptized?" And Philip said, "If you believe with all your heart you may." And he replied, "I believe that Jesus Christ is the Son of God."
—Act 8:26-37 (HCSB)

During a disaster relief deployment, the Billy Graham Rapid Response chaplains attended church services Sunday morning and then left for an afternoon of relaxation and sightseeing. They traveled to a state park not too far from the town of Minot, North Dakota.

While there, they parked the car to look out over the water but then saw prairie dogs close by. The cute little mammals were popping up out of their burrows.

Walking over to read the signage about them, the chaplains saw an elderly man sitting in his car. One of them walked over and started to talk to him about the strange little animals. He told them he came every day to count the prairie dogs and that some of them seemed to be missing today. He mused that the rangers must be "thinning out the litter." He seemed lonely; this was the highlight of his days.

Then he started to share his life, telling the chaplains that when he was a young man, he was a well digger. He said his health was failing him as the years passed by, for you see, he would be eighty-seven years old in a week, on September 1. They asked about his family, and he said his wife of many years had been dead for several years and he had no children.

He said he had a routine every day of driving through the little village and then out to the park to see if anything had changed. He did share that he went to the little church in town on occasion, but then he made his daily rounds.

The chaplains asked him if he knew he would go to heaven when he died, and he said he sure hoped so, but he did not really know. A chaplain explained, "Jesus died for us so we can know we have eternal life, if we ask Him."

The gentleman smiled and said he attended church frequently, but he was still not sure of eternity. He said no one had ever told him he could *know* where he would spend eternity. They showed him the simple prayer in the *Steps to Peace* booklet and told him, "If you believe Jesus died for you and rose again, all you have left to do to be sealed with the blood of Christ is to pray. Would you like to do that?"

Sitting in his car, this soon-to-be eighty-seven-year-old man, with tears running down his wrinkled cheeks, bowed his head and prayed to receive Jesus.

He then smiled at the chaplains and said, "I don't know why you are here today, but I sure am glad you are."

We are often in places that God has designated to be His time and His place. We thought we were traveling to see the sights and the area around us for relaxing in Him. But you see, God knew who would be there and had the timing just right for His Spirit to start working before we arrived. It was the prayers that had been heard and the leading of the Holy Spirit, even though no one knew the circumstances, not even the ones involved. God knew, and that was all that mattered. He knew there was a soul that was searching, and He provided.

How has God provided for you and those you love? Look to Him, giving Him honor and praise. He knows and He sees. He provides.

Chapter 26

SCHEDULED FOR SALVATION

> Jesus said to her, "I am the resurrection and the life. He who
> believes in me will live, even though he dies; and whoever lives
> and believes in me will never die. Do you believe this?"
> —John 11:25-26 (NIV)

Volunteers were few and the job orders were many. Other faith-based organizations often work alongside Samaritan's Purse, and Samaritan's Purse had given one of those teams seventeen work orders out of its stack.

The following week, a homeowner came to the disaster relief unit office to see when Samaritan's Purse could be there to do the work. She was told her work order had been given to the other team. She broke down in tears, as if she had no hope.

The Samaritan's Purse office manager called for a Billy Graham Rapid Response chaplain. The chaplain immediately went to the disaster relief office and started to talk with the lady to calm her. Listening to her and seeing how upset she was, they felt there was more here than just the house and asked the woman about her family.

The lady started to share that she and her husband were raising their three-year-old granddaughter because her father was in prison for abuse and the mother was gone. This homeowner shared she could not forgive the father for what he had done to her daughter and granddaughter.

The Samaritan's Purse office manager and chaplain prayed with the woman and told her only through Jesus could she forgive him, but with Jesus, all things are possible. The chaplain told her that they were going to ask her to do something that might be very difficult for her. They asked her to pray, right then, for the father and then continue to pray for him three times a day. She hesitated for a few moments, but then in tears, she started to pray for him.

A day passed.

The office manager had told the chaplain that she had given the work orders to the other team and did not know the status of this homeowner, because hers was in the stack that had been given to them. The chaplain and office manager prayed together in the Samaritan's Purse truck that God's will would be done and He would get glory.

Another day went by.

As God would have it, the other team came back to the disaster relief unit with the seventeen job orders, saying they were not going to be able to get to them with their low number of volunteers. The office manager looked down, and the lady's job order was on top!

The office manager called the chaplain to share that the job order was back in the hands of Samaritan's Purse. Getting together once again, they had special prayer over this home and the homeowners.

A few days later, this job site was given to a team. Some of the Billy Graham Rapid Response chaplains heard that the homeowner was going to be there when the team arrived, so they went to the home to be there as well. As it turned out, the SP team decided to stop by another job en route and was later getting to this site.

The chaplains came down the road and saw the homeowner waiting on the team in the driveway. (The SP team would not be arriving for forty-five minutes.) She told the chaplains she was faithfully praying for the man (the father of the child) three times a day, as a chaplain had requested her to do.

Then the husband arrived at the scene and the chaplains had the opportunity to build a relationship with him as well. The SP team arrived and was warm and gracious and full of the love of Christ. The team suited up in their Tyveks and went to work in the basement of the house. It overwhelmed both the husband and wife.

The Billy Graham Rapid Response chaplains spoke to the couple about eternal life. They both listened as the gospel of Christ was shared. The husband prayed, for the first time in his life, to receive Christ. The wife prayed and rededicated her life to Christ. The peace that was there was the presence of God.

It was with great joy and celebration that the wife and the little granddaughter came to share dinner with the chaplains and the SP teams that night. The chaplains prepared a dinner to go for the husband who was at work.

God had scheduled this meeting with this job order. Many played a part in this, but He gets the glory!

God's hand was all over this salvation. He always is there, but it was so apparent how these events had been orchestrated for His Word to be shared, uninterrupted.

This reminds me of the song written by a dear friend, Aaron Wilburn, "When God's Four Days Late, He's still on Time." God's timing in our lives is always perfect. It is when we try to get ahead of God that we mess things up. We should always be in prayer, asking for guidance in all things.

Pray and ask Him to give wisdom and direction in your life for any decisions you need to make.

Chapter 27

A SAD CELEBRATION

> But Jesus said, "Let the children alone, and do not hinder them from coming to Me; for the kingdom of heaven belongs to such as these."
> —Matthew 19:14 (NASB)

The Billy Graham Rapid Response chaplains were requested to attend the funeral of a ten-year-old little boy, who was a member of their host church, First Assembly of God, in Minot North Dakota. The little boy had been killed riding a four-wheeler that crashed into a fence. The mother was a single mom. The little boy, Joshua, and the other children were visiting their father in Canada when this accident happened.

By being present in this celebration of a little one's short life, we can see how he and his family influenced the community and the church. Several rows of young boys, Josh's age, filed in with their families.

Josh loved westerns, his favorite television show being *Bonanza*. The family came in, all dressed in western attire, following the tiny casket on which a cowboy hat and his little cowboy boots were sitting. The celebration of Joshua going to heaven was presented in video, showing his youthful antics as well as his baptism earlier in the year. The service was full of his favorite praise songs and "Jesus Loves Me."

As the service ended and the casket started to be rolled out, followed by the family, the theme song of *Bonanza* was played, as if little Joshua were riding off into the sunset to meet Jesus.

We all know there is a time to live and a time to die. We know this precious child had made his preparation for his meeting with Jesus, by his testimony of baptism earlier that year. We need to all think about the time when we will meet Jesus. Are we ready? Do we have our testimony of the day we repented of our sin and accepted Him? "For the Kingdom of heaven belongs to such as these" (Matthew 19:14b).

Little Joshua looking upward to heaven

Chapter 28

WAIT UPON THE LORD

"Yet those who wait for the Lord will gain new strength;
They will mount up with wings like eagles, They will run and
not get tired, They will walk and not become weary."
—Isaiah 40:31 (NASB)

Sometimes, the Billy Graham Rapid Response chaplains are sent out without the Samaritan's Purse Disaster Relief team. One of those times was after Hurricane Gustav came through New Orleans, Louisiana. Power outages and evacuations had caused food to spoil, so the state of Louisiana was issuing emergency food stamps. The people were standing in line for blocks in the heat that rose above one hundred degrees. Tempers were flaring and the national guard had been called to the city. However, things were not improving. The city called the Charlotte, North Carolina, office to see if the Billy Graham Rapid Response chaplains could bring a presence of calmness.

There were about five chaplains sent out, and they began offering bottled water, along with a smile and sometimes a prayer. People were receptive to the chaplains and shared life's problems. They accepted prayers while standing in the lines.

A few days passed, and the lines shortened and began moving at a faster pace. Some of chaplains were sent back home, but a couple remained.

Seeing the situation was dissolving, the couple felt it was time to leave also, especially since Hurricane Ike was fast approaching Galveston, Texas. Samaritan's Purse had already pulled out relief units to stage for the hurricane. However, the chaplain couple had not received the word from the deployment manager to leave New Orleans.

The chaplains had been staying at a church that was located in an old strip mall, which had been flooded in Katrina. It was in the Ninth Ward area and gunshots often could be heard.

The chaplains decided to leave the distribution area, since not much was going on, and to head back to the church to start preparing to leave. One of the chaplains stated, "We need to go toward Galveston or go home, not just sit around here!"

About that time, the other chaplain noticed, through the plateglass window, a "gang" of young boys standing on the sidewalk near the locked door of the church. She told her husband, "I am going out to talk to those boys." He told her to go ahead. He would watch her.

As she approached the young men with tattoos, piercings, chains, and spiked collars, one of them noticed her shirt. He walked toward her and asked, "Is that Billy Graham, the TV preacher?" She smiled and said, "Yes, do you know him?" He said he used to watch Billy Graham on television with his grandmother.

The young man then asked, "Do you believe that stuff?" "What stuff?" the chaplain asked. "The stuff about where you go when you die," said the young man. The chaplain told the young man that she believed she would go to heaven when she died, because of Who she believed in and what He did for her.

Noticing the other young men had quietly disappeared, the chaplain then asked him where he would go when he died. The young man hung his head and somberly replied, "In the ground."

He Goes Before Us

The chaplain asked if he believed in Jesus and knew that He had died on the cross for our sins, and then the chaplain shared with him the *Steps to Peace* booklet.

Johnny said he did believe that, but he also knew he was a sinner. The chaplain told him how Jesus came to die for all sin, even his. Johnny listened and then, with the chaplain's guidance, prayed to receive Christ as Lord and Savior.

The chaplain took Johnny inside to meet her husband and give him a Bible. Johnny hugged them both and thanked them for being there.

Johnny went back outside, looking at his new Bible. After only a few moments, the chaplain saw Johnny on his cell phone and he was motioning for her to come outside. She went out and he was grief stricken, saying, "My friend that was here just got shot in the head. He is still alive!"

The police and ambulance passed the parking lot as he was talking. The chaplain ran inside and got her husband. Johnny said, "I know who did it. I know why they did it, and I know what I must do."

The chaplain told him, "Son, you are a new creature in Christ. He will take care of things for you now. You can't do what you are talking about now."

Moments later, the young pastor of the church pulled into the parking lot. Chaplains introduced Johnny, telling the pastor about his prayer of salvation and his friend who had been shot. The chaplains and the pastor prayed for Johnny and his friends.

After the prayer, Johnny looked at the chaplain and asked, "You know that little booklet *Steps to Peace* you showed me? Can I have about eight of them? I am going to the hospital and my friends will be there."

The chaplain ran inside and got a handful to give to Johnny.

When Johnny left, the chaplains went back inside. After no more than fifteen minutes, the chaplains received a call from the

Billy Graham Rapid Response Team deployment office. They were dismissed from New Orleans and requested to head to Galveston.

(Ginger and her husband saw these things, so that God may be glorified.)

Nothing surprises God. He knows the hearts of man. He also uses men and women to plant the seeds of salvation, and to harvest. He had used this grandmother to plant and set the example of sharing Jesus in her home. Then this young man was passing this experience on to those he loved: his friends. We know one day that the grandmother will see the face of Jesus and will then know that these things came to past.

Please pray today for the youth in our country, that they will be able to see Jesus in all of us. Let us not grow weary. Let us soar like eagles, sharing the joy of the Lord.

How can you plant a seed in someone you love?

Chapter 29

A CHRISTMAS BELL

> "For to us a child is born, to us a son is given, and the government will be on his shoulders. And he will be called Wonderful Counselor, Mighty God, Everlasting Father, Prince of Peace."
> —Isaiah 9:6 (NIV)

After the earthquake in Haiti, Billy Graham Rapid Response Team chaplains responded immediately. After all the pain and heartache, the chaplains were able to bring comfort and peace to many broken hearts.

Months after the earthquake, Cholera became another wave of pain for the Haitian people. Doctors and nurses from all over the world came to Haiti to offer support and aid any way they could. The response of caring people flowed into the already hurting island.

The rapid response chaplains were there for the medical staff; many were seeing death looking them straight in the eyes for the first time. The chaplains were having devotions and prayer with the medical teams, as they were leaving the base camp going to the clinics for long, fourteen-hour shifts. The chaplains were there to greet them when the emotional and physically drained teams returned to camp.

On Christmas Eve, the chaplains planned special services, which included the Lord's Supper of Kool-Aid and graham crackers and singing of Christmas carols. As one of the songs concluded, a chaplain thought, *Did I just hear a Christmas bell?* She thought that maybe it was a little goat eating grass nearby, but then she realized the goats did not have bells.

At the end of the service, the chaplain turned to the head nurse, Debi, who had been sitting next to her, when she saw the Christmas bell with a red ribbon tied around Debi's neck. She laughed and told Debi that she thought she had heard "an angel get its wings" when she heard the bell.

Debi left with the medical team for a very busy night of cholera patients coming into the makeshift hospital of tents. The rest of Debi's story follows.

> As I stood in line to wash my hands about 2 a.m., I noted a pregnant woman ahead of me in line. A query revealed that she was a visitor, the wife of a patient, so I went on about my work. I was helping a very dehydrated woman whose jaw repeatedly dislocated, starting difficult IVs, answering questions, acting as a provider in the pediatric area, and providing backup in the busy admitting triage tent.
>
> A few hours later, the excited voice of our sole expatriate doctor called out, "Debi, come here. We have a woman in labor!" Quickly responding, I saw our pregnant visitor panting and clutching her stomach. Fortunately, one of our Haitian physicians was an OB/GYN and examined the patient, who was now in full-blown labor.
>
> "Do we have time to transfer her?" I frantically asked, repeatedly dialing the phone of the Red Cross ambulance service. No one answered.
>
> "No, her contractions are too close," the doctor said. "Plus no ambulances or *tap taps* (local

public transportation) are going to be working on Christmas!"

We rushed the woman into a small, unused corner of the CTC, hanging blankets over the wooden posts in a makeshift attempt at privacy. Besides our OB/GYN physician, the delivery team included a paramedic, a nurse working pediatrics that had neonatal ICU experience, and the young American resident doctor.

Rapidly, I scoured the pharmacy and came up with a very few basic supplies—some sterile instruments, a large syringe with tubing attached for a suction device, a very large diaper to cover the infant—and gathered the clean, freshly laundered, non-cholera sheets and blankets that we had brought along for naps. The only thing missing was a cord clamp or twill tape to tie off the umbilical cord.

"Samantha" was delivered at 6 a.m., healthy and crying. Dad also cried—tears of joy—as he sat propped at Mama's bedside, holding her hand as he continued to receive IV fluids in the other arm.

Despite our attempts at privacy, this was a CTC event and the female patients that were strong enough to stand and walk had clustered around the area, clapping and cheering as soon as baby cried.

The physician held out his hand for the umbilical clamp, and I gave him the only thing I had available: the red silken cord from the Christmas angel bell necklace! It worked well, and soon baby was suctioned and dried, resting on Mom's chest beneath a clean blanket. Dad, tottering from weakness and exhaustion, was helped back to his bed to continue cholera treatment and recovery.

We went back to the base that day, exhausted yet exhilarated. We had seen death, then life. An unexpected birth—a Christmas child—and we were there to give witness. To help beat back the forces of death that threatened to overwhelm the Haitian people, who had already suffered so much loss. To give up so little—simply a holiday—compared to what He had given up for us.

We were there to help a precious little child to be born safe and healthy to loving parents, in the middle of a ravaged and destroyed country, during a cholera epidemic. We were there to give hope on a very special Christmas night.

Another nurse shared with the chaplains that they had cut a hole in the center of an adult diaper and pulled it over the baby's head. The team found some gauze, wrapped it around the little one's head, and tied a big bow to help keep her warm. This was truly another babe wrapped in swaddling clothes on Christmas night.

That night was a true reminder to all of us how really special Christmas is. Christmas is a time to reflect on how big God really is, from a small baby being born in Bethlehem to another baby born in a third-world country that many traveled from all over the world to witness.

How does God show His greatness to you, especially at Christmas?

Chapter 30

A CHILD SHALL LEAD THEM

"And a little child shall lead them."
—Isaiah 11:6 (NIV)

One day, while visiting a homeowner, Billy Graham Rapid Response chaplains met other family members. One was a precious grandson watching his grandmother as she handled this situation of the storm damage.

As the chaplain sat down in the floor with the eight-year-old, he started to tell what he remembered about the night of the tornado. With big, excited eyes that recalled fear, he pointed to the place where the family had huddled together when they heard the storm coming. Then, almost in awe, Timothy looked straight at and chaplain and said, "If I had died, I don't know what would have happened!"

Looking over at the grandmother, who was standing across the room and listening, the chaplain asked, "May I share with your grandson?"

With tears starting to roll down her rounded, dark cheeks, she smiled and nodded a firm yes.

The chaplain started to tell Timothy that Jesus loved him and that Jesus had died for him. But Timothy interrupted the chaplain, saying he knew about Jesus because his grandmother had told him.

Timothy listened as the story of what he had heard for many years became real to him—that God did love him enough to send His Son, Jesus, to die for him. If he wanted to, since he believed and trusted about Jesus, he could pray and receive Him as his Savior and never have to wonder what would happen if he died. This is because Jesus promises us an eternal home in heaven, to live with Him forever and ever.

Timothy asked if he could pray to make sure he would go to heaven. All of the people in the room bowed their heads as this little precious boy, praying in the voice of an eight-year-old, with the gentle whispered sobs of a grandmother in the background, asked Jesus to forgive him and come into his heart.

At the end, Timothy said, "Amen."

The chaplain got up on her knees to hug him and heard a thundering voice from above her.

"Excuse me, ma'am, but I am his uncle. Can I do the same thing and pray that prayer too?" The uncle was a very large, thirty-year-old, muscled, dark man standing above them.

From somewhere off, the grandmother was saying, "Glory to God in the highest!"

We serve an awesome God that hears and answers the prayers of the saints. This precious grandmother not only shared her knowledge of Jesus with those around her but also lived her walk with Him before them. The respect and love for her was seen not only in the family but also in the community.

Do the people you meet on a daily basis see Jesus in you?

Chapter 31

REDEDICATIONS AND RENEWAL OF WALKING WITH CHRIST

> "Draw nigh to God, and He will draw nigh to you."
> —James 4:8 (KJV)

Chaplains visited elderly owners of a house and listened to their story of the night of the tornado. The owners also shared that they had two daughters die at the young ages of seventeen and thirty-three. During the storm, while huddled in the bathroom, they talked of their daughters. The man had looked at his wife, when they heard the house coming apart, and said, "We are not going to make it through this one."

The chaplains asked, "If you had not made it, do you know where you were going?"

The wife said, "Hopefully to see my daughters." She said they all had joined and been baptized at a church several years ago but had not attended in many years. The Billy Graham Rapid Response chaplains led them in a prayer of rededication and gave the husband and wife some Christian materials. They both said they wanted to walk close with the Lord again, so they could have peace.

* * *

Chaplains visited another homeowner, in the same area, and met her son and granddaughters. The chaplains felt led to ask the son if he attended church, and he replied, "No, but my wife goes." When asked if he knew where he would spend eternity after he died, he replied, "I am not sure. I've done some bad things." But he did say that he had committed his life to Christ at a young age.

After sharing the hope and security of Jesus, chaplains led him in a prayer of rededication.

When you renew your vow to the Lord or rededicate, you are making a heartfelt decision communicated to God through prayer. People generally rededicate their lives to the Lord for one of two reasons.

- They once enjoyed walking with the Lord, but for whatever reason, a gap or separation occurred in their relationship and they now desire to walk with Him again.

  1 John 1:9: "If we confess our sins, He is faithful and just to forgive us our sins, and to cleanse us from all unrighteousness."

- They have continued to walk with the Lord; however, they desire a closer, more intimate walk Him.

Where are you in your walk with the Lord? Has sin placed a gap in your relationship with Him? Begin walking anew with Him today, looking to Him for peace and hope in your life. He always promises to hear our prayers and to be with us. Let Him be your friend today.

Peace with God

Do you know the peace and the abundant life that God planned for you?
"We have peace with God through our Lord Jesus Christ" (Romans 5:1).
"For God so loved the world that he gave his one and only Son, that whoever believes in him shall not perish but have eternal life" (John 3:16).
"I have come that they may have life, and that they may have it more abundantly" (John 10:10 NKJV).

We are separated from God because of sin.
"For all have sinned and fall short of the glory of God" (Romans 3:23).
"For the wages of sin is death, but the gift of God is eternal life in Christ Jesus our Lord" (Romans 6:23NKJV).

Though many try different ways to reach God, there is only one way.
"There is a way that seems right to a man, but in the end it leads to death" (Proverbs 14:12).

God has provided the only way, and we each must choose.
"For Christ died for sins once for all, the righteous for the unrighteous, to bring you to God" (1 Peter 3:18).
"For there is one God and one mediator between God and men, the man Christ Jesus" (1 Timothy 2:5).

**We must trust Jesus Christ and receive
Him as our Lord and Savior.**
"That if you confess with your mouth, 'Jesus is Lord,'
and believe in your heart that God raised him from
the dead, you will be saved" (Romans 10:9).
"Yet to all who received him, to those who believed in his name,
he gave the right to become children of God" (John 1:12).

Would you like to receive Christ right now?
- Admit you are a sinner. (I am a sinner.)
- Be willing to turn from your sins. (Repent.)
- Believe Jesus died for you on the cross and arose from the grave.

If you have done those three things, the only thing left to do is to pray and invite Jesus into your heart.

This is a sample prayer:

> Dear Lord Jesus,
> I know that I am a sinner. I am sorry, and I ask for Your forgiveness. I do believe You died on the cross for me and rose from the dead. Turning from my sins, I invite You into my heart and life, filling me with Your Holy Spirit and be my Lord and Savior.
> In Your Name,
> Amen.

If you prayed that prayer, think of someone who would like to know about this decision and be sure to let them know. It could be someone who has been praying for you for many years.

If you have prayed this prayer and are seeking more information, please go to www.KnowingGod.net and www.GoingFarther.net.

Also, go to www.gingersanders.com and let me know of your decision, so I can pray for you.

But don't stop here. Begin your new walk with Jesus Christ today. The journey is abundant, as He has promised. This does not mean that you will not have trials and tribulations in this world; we still live in a sinful world. But He does promise in his Word that He will be with us.

2 Corinthians 1:4: "Who gives us comfort in all our troubles, so that we may be able to give comfort to others who are in trouble, through the comfort with which we ourselves are comforted by God."

Peace and blessings as you go on your journey. And remember your future is His memory, because *He Goes before Us*.

Ginger Sanders

Afterword

As we look back at all the times we have seen God working in so many different situations and in so many lives, we are reminded that nothing surprises God. He is prepared to meet every need in every situation.

The Billy Graham Rapid Response Team had been to Fort Collins and Colorado Springs, Colorado, for the fires, working alongside Samaritan's Purse volunteers as they sifted through ashes. These worksites were located just north and south of Denver, respectively. Billy Graham Rapid Response chaplains were called from both locations to the Aurora, Colorado, theater shooting, arriving at the local high school to be with families, friends, and first responders within hours of this tragedy. Sometimes praying, sometimes listening, and sometimes just sitting and holding a hand or simply bringing a cup of coffee to a loved one. God's presence was there. He knew the heartbreak the community was going through.

Only months later, God once again seemingly placed the Billy Graham Rapid Response chaplains prior to a horrific incident. Hurricane Sandy had hit the east coast with brutal force. Samaritan's Purse sent teams out and the chaplains were working with them. Chaplains were on Long Island, New York, and another team was in Toms River, New Jersey, when they received a call to go immediately to Sandy Hook, Connecticut.

Within hours, the Billy Graham Rapid Response chaplains were on the scene to be with the small community that was hurting.

Chaplains were there to let not only the family, friends, and first responders know that God loved them in the midst of the tragedy, but to let others know as well.

Members of the media had arrived by the number and were staying at the hotels where chaplains were staying. Several times, the crew or reporter would come to the RRT chaplains with tears running down their cheeks. You see, God loves everyone, and in deep times of pain, His love is felt. Prayers were prayed not only with the local community; others came from hours away to attend memorials and pray even in elevators, requesting a prayer or word of encouragement.

We live in hard times. We all need to encourage each other with prayer and lift each other up. The Devil would like nothing else than for us to be discouraged with this world which we live in and to quit serving God. But we know, without a shadow of a doubt, because we have seen these things, that He is alive and well. *He Goes before Us.*

Acronyms

BGEA   Billy Graham Evangelistic Association
BG   Billy Graham
RRT   Rapid Response Team
SP   Samaritan's Purse
DR   Disaster Relief

About the Author

Ginger Sanders was born and raised in north Alabama. She grew up on a farm, learning how to drive in the middle of a hayfield. She was raised in a home that believed in Christ, and that is what gives her the hope of seeing her parents and sister who are already in heaven. Ginger was brought up in a home filled with Southern hospitality, where cooking and serving others was expected. She enjoys friends and family times together but also enjoys being out on the mission field, whether domestically or in a foreign land.

She retired from her job in the world of finance and returned to the roots that grounded her: serving others. She and her husband have trained and served with the Billy Graham Evangelistic Association and now serve with the Billy Graham Rapid Response Team as chaplain coordinators. They are called to disasters, natural and manmade, to give emotional and spiritual care.

Ginger has traveled extensively, speaking at women's conferences, youth conferences, retreats, and various events. She has led many different Bible studies and classes for men, women, and youth. One of the things most important to her is being able to see people grow in the Lord. But, more importantly, that they know Christ and have a personal relationship with Him.

She gives God glory for all the things He has allowed her to witness, knowing it was Him and Him alone that provided the love and resources. She has learned never to give up on God and that He is always there with His child. One of her best-known sayings—"It was a God thing!"—has been proven over and over, and it still amazes her.

Ginger is married to her high school sweetheart, Denny. They adopted two children from South Korea—Jamie and Kara—and then had two biological children: Todd and B.J. Ginger prayed for mates for their children, while they were still young, and feels so blessed with their three daughters-in-laws and son-in-law that God has put into the family. They are blessed with ten grandchildren, who are spread out across the United States. However, Ginger looks forward to the family get-togethers at their lakeside home in Alabama.

She has been writing for several years and has written a children's book, Round Eyes, based on the true story of when their little boy from Korea realized he looked different. God answered prayers in bringing all of their children to them.

You may contact Ginger on twitter @gingersanders, on facebook or at her website www. gingersanders.com

CPSIA information can be obtained
at www.ICGtesting.com
Printed in the USA
LVOW04s0532071216
516161LV00010BA/183/P

9 781498 459471